A Grandmother's Book

By

_____

Grandmother's Name

_____

(Date of Birth)

_____

(Place of Birth)

All Scripture quotations, unless otherwise specified, are taken from the King James Version of the Bible. (Copyright © 1982 by Holman Bible Publishers. All rights reserved.)

Scripture quotations noted NKJV are from the *Holy Bible*, New King James Version, (Copyright © 1979, 1980, 1982 by Thomas Nelson, Inc. Used by permission. All rights reserved.)

Scripture quotations noted NIV are from the *Holy Bible*, New International Version, (Copyright © 1973, 1978, 1984 by International Bible Society. Used by permission.)

Scripture quotations noted NLT are from the *Holy Bible*, New Living Translation, (Copyright © 1996. Used by permission of Tyndale House Publishers, Inc., Wheaton, Illinois 60189. All rights reserved.)

All rights in this book are reserved world-wide. No part of the book may be reproduced in any manner whatsoever without written permission of the author except in brief quotations embodied in critical articles of reviews.

For information on ordering please contact Vision Publishing, 1115 D Street, Ramona, CA 92065. 1-800-9-VISION.
www.visionpublishingservices.com

Copyright © Victoria Harr 2008

ISBN 1-931178-52-6

DEDICATION

This book is dedicated to all the grandmothers who believe they have a story to share—and you do! It is yours and yours only.

The questions are phrased in such a way that the grandmother is telling the grandchild about her life. They may not know it now, but they will come to appreciate your efforts and cherish your memories even more as time passes.

I suggest you draft your answers before making them permanent in the book. When complete, this will be a treasure *only you* can give your grandchild.

I want to thank my best friend, Jan Moore, for proofing and feedback, our good friend, Bob Sarawinski, for refining the family tree and cover, and for my long-time friends, Karen Castillo, Diane Hamilton, Karen Anderson, Debbie Goosman and their families, for giving me permission to use their photographs on the front cover. I couldn't have done it without all of you.

But most of all, this book is dedicated to all the grandchildren who will receive this gift of love from their grandmother.

INTRODUCTION

Timothy, I thank God for you. He is the God I serve with a clear conscience, just as my ancestors did. Night and day I constantly remember you in my prayers. I long to see you again, for I remember your tears as we parted. And I will be filled with joy when we are together again. I know that you sincerely trust the Lord, for you have the faith of your mother, Eunice, and your grandmother, Lois. This is why I remind you to fan into flames the spiritual gift God gave you when I laid my hands on you. For God has not given us a spirit of fear and timidity, but of power, love, and self-discipline. So you must never be ashamed to tell others about our Lord (II Timothy 1:2-7, NLT).

Just as Paul the Apostle recognized the legacy Timothy had received from his mother and grandmother, my prayer is that your grandchild will receive a spiritual legacy from you—a collection of memories only you can pass on.

There are many baby books on the market for a mother to fill out for her child, but there are fewer for a grandmother. When my mother attempted to find a grandmother's book to fill out for my children, she had to adapt the text by handwriting "grand" in front of mother. So this inspired me to create a grandmother's book that was made specifically for a grandmother and which also had a heavy spiritual emphasis.

My grandchildren like to hear me tell them stories about their parent when their parent was little. They also say "Grandma, tell me a story about when you were a little girl." But as much as I love telling them those stories, there is so much more I want to share that time just simply doesn't seem to allow given our busy lives. This book is another tool you can use to pass on your natural heritage as well as your personal journey of faith.

TABLE OF CONTENTS

	Page No.
Before You Were Born	1

Jeremiah
Ephesians
Isaiah

My Family Tree 3

Events Surrounding My First Year 5

Moses
Samuel
Esau
Jacob

Early Years 15

David

Teenage Years 29

Jeremiah

Young Adult Years 43

Esther

Mature Adult Years 51

Job

Years of Reflection 59

Job

Special Memories 75

Journey of Faith 89

Before You Were Born

A Grandmother's Life, as told to Her Grandchild

A Grandmother's Life, as told to Her Grandchild
Before You Were Born

God's Word in Jeremiah 1:5, NLT says, "I knew you before I formed you in your mother's womb."

God also says that . . . "Long ago, even before he made the world, God loved us and chose us in Christ to be holy and without fault in his eyes," (Ephesians 1:4, NLT) and the Bible also says "For we are God's masterpiece. He has created us anew in Christ Jesus, so that we can do the good things he planned for us long ago" (Ephesians 2:10, NLT).

Finally, Isaiah 43:1, NLT says ". . . the Lord who created you says: '. . . I have called you by name; you are mine.'" That means *even before either you or I were born*, God knew all about us--what we were going to be like, what we were going to look like, (right down to the color of our hair and eyes), our personality and temperament, even who our parents and grandparents were going to be and everything else about us. God decides where and when we are born and who we are born to. What a concept! It's something we have no control over, but God does. God's plan for me was that you'd be my grandchild. I didn't know that when I was younger, but God knew it, and I'm so glad He gave you to me and gave me to you.

Although He created us for Himself first and foremost, He also created us for each other, and He has a plan for each of us. It's mindboggling, isn't it? Not only that, He expects us to find out that plan — to discover our destiny — and He is there all along the way to help us.

My Family Tree

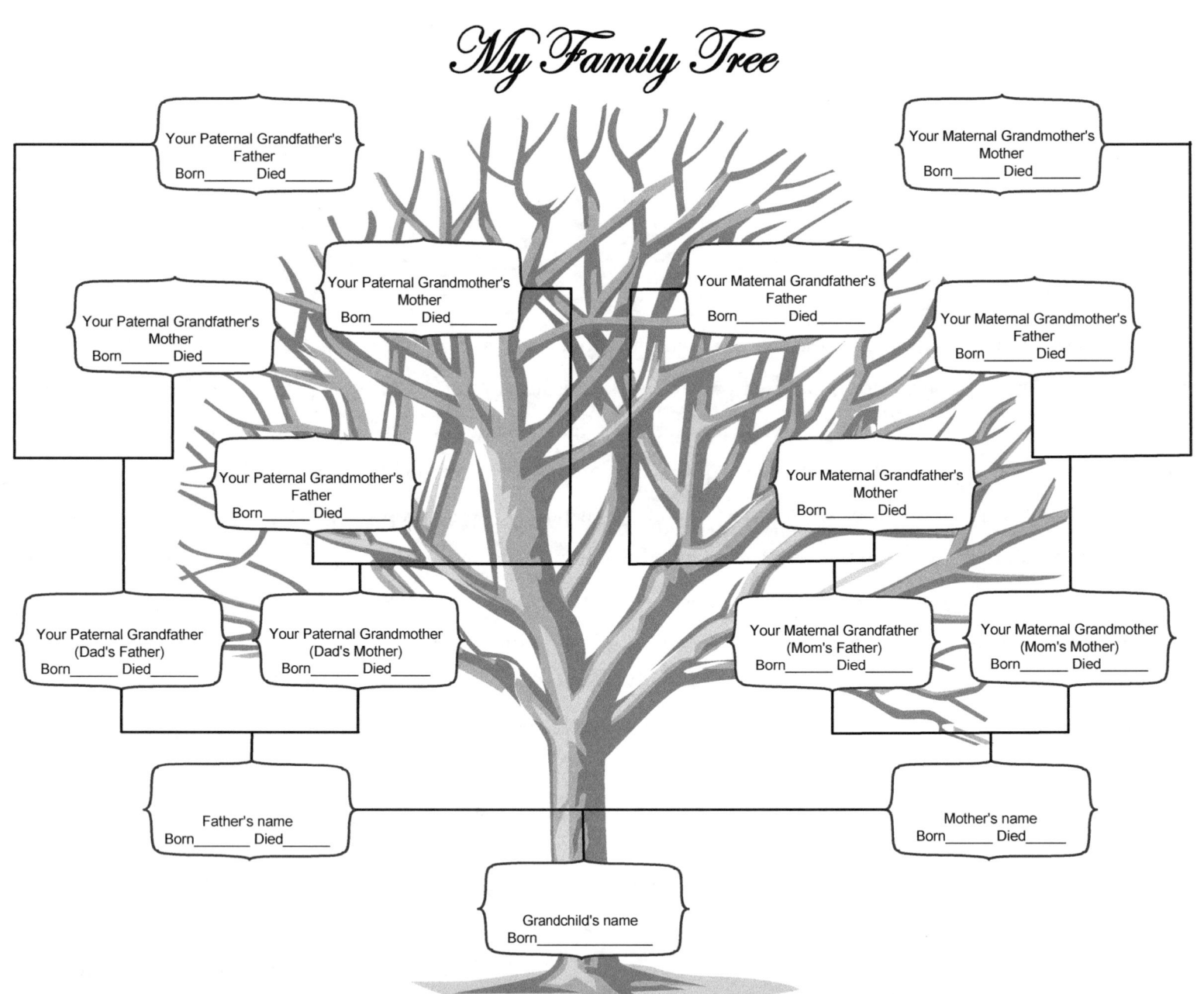

Your Paternal Grandfather's
Father
Born_____ Died_____

Your Maternal Grandmother's
Mother
Born_____ Died_____

Your Paternal Grandmother's
Mother
Born_____ Died_____

Your Maternal Grandfather's
Father
Born_____ Died_____

Your Paternal Grandfather's
Mother
Born_____ Died_____

Your Maternal Grandmother's
Father
Born_____ Died_____

Your Paternal Grandmother's
Father
Born_____ Died_____

Your Maternal Grandfather's
Mother
Born_____ Died_____

Your Paternal Grandfather
(Dad's Father)
Born_____ Died_____

Your Paternal Grandmother
(Dad's Mother)
Born_____ Died_____

Your Maternal Grandfather
(Mom's Father)
Born_____ Died_____

Your Maternal Grandmother
(Mom's Mother)
Born_____ Died_____

Father's name
Born_____ Died_____

Mother's name
Born_____ Died_____

Grandchild's name
Born_____

A Grandmother's Life, as told to Her Grandchild
Before You Were Born

Some characteristics that run through our family which you have inherited are _____

_____

_____

_____

_____

_____

Some characteristics that I notice you have inherited from me are _____

_____

_____

_____

_____

_____

Events Surrounding My First Year

A Grandmother's Life, as told to Her Grandchild

A Grandmother's Life, as told to Her Grandchild
Events Surrounding My First Year

"So God created man in his [own] image, in the image of God created he him; male and female created he them" (Genesis 1:27). Each of us is an original—one-of-a-kind. There's no one like us--and the circumstances surrounding each of our births are unique too. This is a story about a most unusual birth.

During this time, a man and woman from the tribe of Levi got married. The woman became pregnant and gave birth to a son. She saw what a beautiful baby he was and kept him hidden for three months. But when she could no longer hide him, she got a little basket made of papyrus reeds and waterproofed it with tar and pitch. She put the baby in the basket and laid it among the reeds along the edge of the Nile River. The baby's sister then stood at a distance, watching to see what would happen to him. Soon after this, one of Pharaoh's daughters came down to bathe in the river, and her servant girls walked along the riverbank. When the princess saw the little basket among the reeds, she told one of her servant girls to get it for her. As the princess opened it, she found the baby boy. His helpless cries touched her heart. 'He must be one of the Hebrew children,' she said. Then the baby's sister approached the princess. 'Should I go and find one of the Hebrew women to nurse the baby for you?' she asked. 'Yes, do!' the princess replied. So the girl rushed home and called the baby's mother. 'Take this child home and nurse him for me,' the princess told her. 'I will pay you for your help.' So the baby's mother took her baby home and nursed him. Later, when he was older, the child's mother brought him back to the princess, who adopted him as her son. The princess named him Moses, for she said, 'I drew him out of the water' (Exodus 2:1-10, NLT).

I was born on _____ at _____
                               (Date)   (City and State)

I weighed _____pounds and was _____inches long.

At my birth, my hair color was _____ and my eyes were _____.

A Grandmother's Life, as told to Her Grandchild
Events Surrounding My First Year

The most unique thing surrounding my birth was _____

_____

_____

_____

_____

Family members present at my birth were _____

_____

_____

_____

My immediate family consisted of my parent(s) and sibling(s) whose name(s) and age(s) at the time I was born were:

Mother _____

                              (Name)   (Age)

Father _____

                              (Name)   (Age)

A Grandmother's Life, as told to Her Grandchild
Events Surrounding My First Year

Brother _____
                                                      (Name)   (Age)

Brother _____
(Name) (Age)

Sister _____
(Name) (Age)

Sister _____
(Name) (Age)

I was the _____ child in a family of ____. Later other children were born. Their names and ages were:

Brother _____
(Name) (Age)

Brother _____
(Name) (Age)

Sister _____
(Name) (Age)

Sister _____
(Name) (Age)

A Grandmother's Life, as told to Her Grandchild
Events Surrounding My First Year

My parent(s) brought me home to _____
(City/State)

Members of my family described my temperament as being _____

_____

_____

_____

MORE ABOUT MY IMMEDIATE FAMILY: _____

_____

_____

_____

_____

_____

_____

A Grandmother's Life, as told to Her Grandchild
Events Surrounding My First Year

Hebrew children were usually named after a circumstance surrounding their birth, such as when Hannah had her baby boy. She had gone through so much waiting for a baby and had asked the Lord so long for a child, that when he finally arrived, she named him Samuel, which means ". . . Because I have asked him of the Lord" (I Samuel 1:20).

Sometimes they were given a name that "fit them," like Esau whose body was covered with red hair. "And the first came out red, all over like an hairy garment; and they called his name Esau" (Genesis 25:25).

After the Hebrew child was grown, often the names which had been given by the parents to the child were changed by God Himself, who would call them to a higher destiny. This would cause the person to look at the potential of their new name. For instance, God changed Jacob's name which meant "heel holder or a layer of snares,"[1] to Israel, which means "God prevails."[2] And He said, "Your name shall no longer be called Jacob, but Israel; for you have struggled with God and with men, and have prevailed" (Genesis 32:28, NKJV).

Some names reflect ethnic heritages. Our ethnic heritage is _____

However, most parents in our culture pick out names they like or a name that reminds them of a relative or friend they admire. Other parents intentionally pick out Christian or Jewish names after looking up the meaning.

I was named _____
             (First)   (Middle)   (Last)

after _____

---

[1] http://cf.blueletterbible.org/lang/lexicon/lexicon.cfm?Strongs=H03290&Version=kjv. Online posting as of 12/21/07.
[2] http://cf.blueletterbible.org/lang/lexicon/lexicon.cfm?Strongs=H03478&Version=kjv. Online posting as of 12/21/07.

A Grandmother's Life, as told to Her Grandchild
Events Surrounding My First Year

My name means _____

_____

My parents chose my name because _____

_____

_____

Later I was nicknamed _____ by _____
                                                                    (Name)

because _____

_____

MORE ABOUT OUR FAMILY'S NAMES: _____

_____

_____

_____

_____

A Grandmother's Life, as told to Her Grandchild
Events Surrounding My First Year

MORE ABOUT MY FIRST YEAR: _____

_____

_____

_____

_____

_____

_____

_____

_____

_____

_____

_____

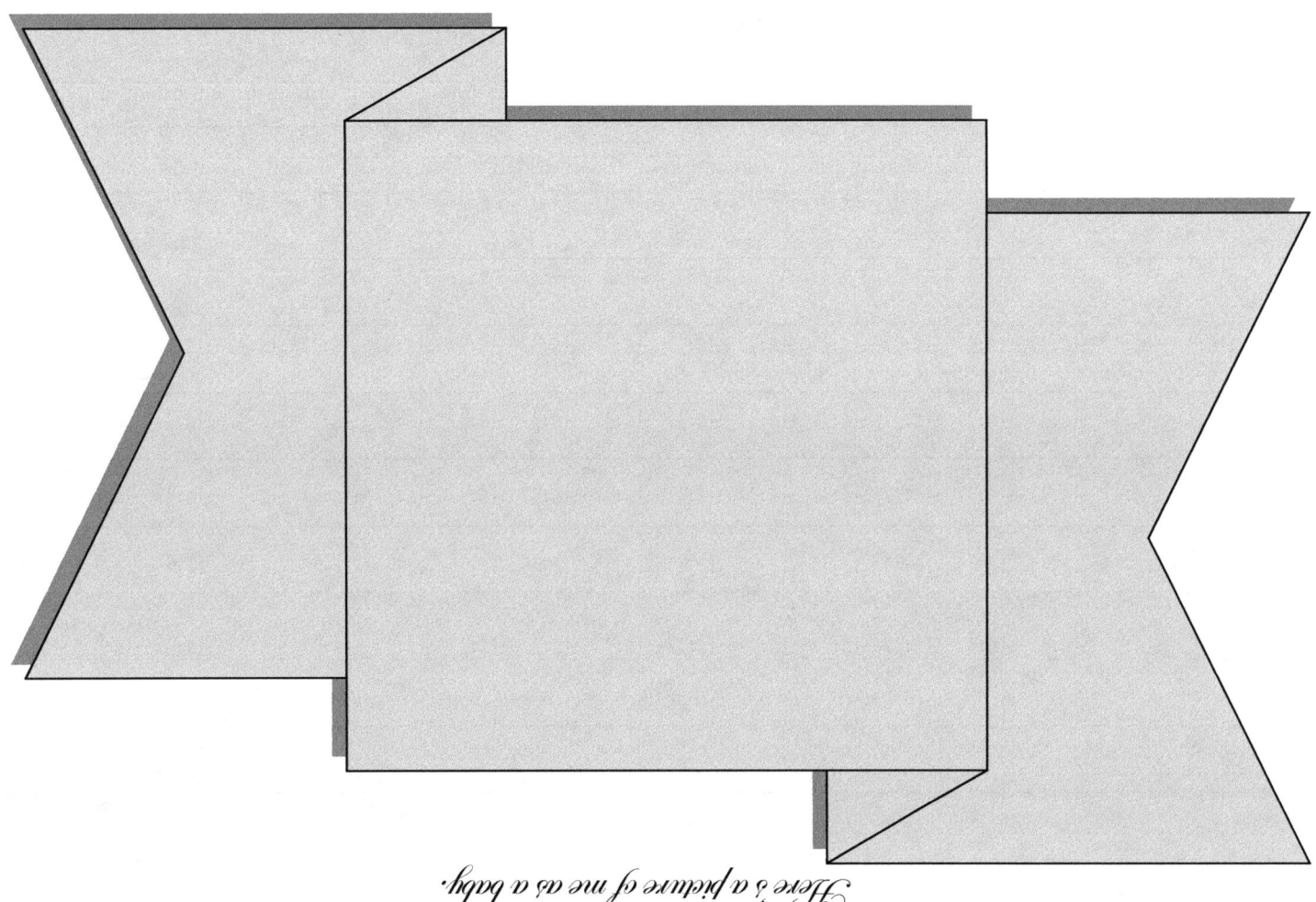

Grandmother's Life, as told to Her Grandchild
Events Surrounding My First Year

Here's a picture of me as a baby.

A Grandmother's Life, as told to Her Grandchild
Events Surrounding My First Year

Early Years

A Grandmother's Life, as told to Her Grandchild

A Grandmother's Life, as told to Her Grandchild
Early Years

When we are young, we often imagine or dream of what we want to become when we "grow up." Sometimes our dreams come true, but more often than not they take a surprising turn, and we find our lives going in an unexpected direction.

One such young man was named David. Born into a family of seven brothers, he was a musician and especially liked to play the harp out in the hills of Bethlehem while he tended sheep. As the youngest, he thought he was going to be a shepherd his entire life. But God had another plan for his life. Here is how David's idea of what his life would be like was unexpectedly changed by God.

> The Lord said to Samuel, ". . . I am sending you to Jesse of Bethlehem. I have chosen one of his sons to be king." . . . The Lord said, ". . . Invite Jesse to the sacrifice, and I will show you what to do. You are to anoint for me the one I indicate." Samuel did what the Lord said. . . . Then he consecrated Jesse and his sons and invited them to the sacrifice. When they arrived, Samuel saw Eliab and thought, "Surely the Lord's anointed stands here before the Lord." But the Lord said to Samuel, "Do not consider his appearance or his height, for I have rejected him. The Lord does not look at the things man looks at. Man looks at the outward appearance, but the Lord looks at the heart." Then Jesse called Abinadab and had him pass in front of Samuel. But Samuel said, "The Lord has not chosen this one either." Jesse then had Shammah pass by, but Samuel said, "Nor has the Lord chosen this one." Jesse had seven of his sons pass before Samuel, but Samuel said to him, "The Lord has not chosen these." So he asked Jesse, "Are these all the sons you have?" "There is still the youngest," Jesse answered, "but he is tending the sheep." Samuel said, "Send for him; we will not sit down until he arrives." So he sent and had him brought in. He was ruddy, with a fine appearance and handsome features. Then the Lord said, "Rise and anoint him; he is the one." So Samuel took the horn of oil and anointed him in the presence of his brothers, and from that day on the Spirit of the Lord came upon David in power (I Samuel 6:1-13, NIV).

A Grandmother's Life, as told to Her Grandchild
Early Years

Soon, David found himself in the court of King Saul, playing the harp for the King instead of the sheep. Then he was promoted to be Saul's armor bearer and served on the King's staff. He did not become King until many years later. As a young man, he had no idea his life would turn out that way.

Now the Spirit of the Lord had left Saul, and the Lord sent a tormenting spirit that filled him with depression and fear. Some of Saul's servants suggested a remedy. "It is clear that a spirit from God is tormenting you," they said. "Let us find a good musician to play the harp for you whenever the tormenting spirit is bothering you. The harp music will quiet you, and you will soon be well again." "All right," Saul said. "Find me someone who plays well and bring him here." One of the servants said to Saul, "The son of Jesse is a talented harp player. Not only that; he is brave and strong and has good judgment. He is also a fine-looking young man, and the Lord is with him." So Saul sent messengers to Jesse to say, "Send me your son David, the shepherd." Jesse responded by sending David to Saul, along with a young goat and a donkey loaded down with food and wine. So David went to Saul and served him. Saul liked David very much, and David became one of Saul's armor bearers. Then Saul sent word to Jesse asking, "Please let David join my staff, for I am very pleased with him." And whenever the tormenting spirit from God troubled Saul, David would play the harp. Then Saul would feel better, and the tormenting spirit would go away (I Samuel 16:14-23, NLT).

The story above is a good example of how God works in our lives, often without us knowing it. "A man's heart plans his way, but the Lord directs his steps (Proverbs 16:9, NKJV). Looking back, many times I have been surprised at how God was working behind the scenes in my life.

A Grandmother's Life, as told to Her Grandchild
Early Years

In my early years, I dreamed that when I grew up I would be _____

_____

_____

_____

I went to elementary school(s) in _____
(City and State)

_____

My best friend was _____

and some of the things we did together were _____

_____

_____

_____

_____

A Grandmother's Life, as told to Her Grandchild
Early Years

My favorite subjects/classes during elementary school were _____

_____

_____

_____

_____

_____

and my favorite teachers were _____

_____

_____

_____

_____

A Grandmother's Life, as told to Her Grandchild
Early Years

People told me some of my natural talents were _____

_____

_____

_____

_____

Some instruments I played during my early years were _____

_____

_____

_____

_____

People who taught me to play those instruments and/or musical classes I took during this time were _____

_____

_____

_____

A Grandmother's Life, as told to Her Grandchild
Early Years

Some of my favorite activities during elementary school were _____

_____

_____

_____

Some of the sports I participated in during elementary school were _____

_____

_____

_____

After school, I spent my time _____

_____

_____

_____

A Grandmother's Life, as told to Her Grandchild
Early Years

Some of my chores at home were _____

_____

_____

_____

The chore(s) I disliked the most were _____

_____

_____

_____

I received my first allowance of _____ when I was _____ years old for doing _____
  (Amount)

_____

_____

_____

A Grandmother's Life, as told to Her Grandchild
Early Years

I received my last allowance when I was _____ years old because _____

_____

_____

_____

_____

My most beloved toy was _____

because _____

_____

_____

_____

_____

A Grandmother's Life, as told to Her Grandchild
Early Years

My favorite book was _____

_____

because _____

_____

_____

_____

I lost my first tooth when I was _____ years old. When a child lost a tooth in our family, our tradition was to _____

_____

_____

_____

_____

A Grandmother's Life, as told to Her Grandchild
Early Years

My most anticipated TV program was _____

_____

_____

_____

One of the radio programs I listened to most were _____

_____

_____

My pets were _____

_____

_____

_____

_____

MORE ABOUT MY EARLY YEARS:

My Grandmother's Life, as told to Her Grandchild
Early Years

Here's a picture of me as a young child.

A Grandmother's Life, as told to Her Grandchild

Teenage Years

A Grandmother's Life, as told to Her Grandchild

A Grandmother's Life, as told to Her Grandchild
Teenage Years

The word of the Lord came to me, saying, "Before I formed you in the womb I chose you, before you were born I set you apart; I appointed you as a prophet to the nations." "Ah, Sovereign Lord," I said, "I do not know how to speak; I am only a child." But the Lord said to me, "Do not say, 'I am only a child.' You must go to everyone I send you to and say whatever I command you. Do not be afraid of them, for I am with you and will rescue you," declares the Lord (Jeremiah 1:4-8, NIV).

Jeremiah was a young man, probably between 17 and 25 years old when God personally called him to his life's purpose. He considered himself to be a child, too young to be used by God, and certainly too young to speak on God's behalf. The Hebrew word for "child" should be translated "young man." [3] But no one is ever "too young" or "too old" to be used by God. He can use anyone, any time for His purposes. Although it is unusual for a teenager to have the maturity, wisdom and insight to know what God has chosen for him or her, sometimes the dreams we have inside us are put there by God.

My dreams, aspirations and goals as a teenager were _____

_____

_____

_____

---

[3] http://www.blueletterbible.org/cgi-bin/comm_read.pl?book=Jer&chapter=1&verse=5&Comm=Comm%2Fchuck_smith%2Fsg%2Fjeremiah.html%23ch1@@@@@3%26.Chuck%26Smith&Select.x=25&Select.y=15. Online posting as of 12/21/07.

A Grandmother's Life, as told to Her Grandchild
Teenage Years

I went to high school in _____

(City and State)

As a teenager, my best friend was _____

and some of the things we did together were _____

_____

_____

_____

_____

Some of my favorite subjects in high school were _____

_____

_____

_____

_____

A Grandmother's Life, as told to Her Grandchild
Teenage Years

My favorite teachers were _____

_____

_____

_____

Some of the skills and abilities I was developing were _____

_____

_____

_____

Some instruments I played as a teenager were _____

_____

_____

_____

A Grandmother's Life, as told to Her Grandchild
Teenage Years

People who taught me to play those instruments during this time were _____

_____

_____

_____

_____

Some musical/vocal classes I took as a teenager were _____

_____

_____

Some hobbies I had were _____

_____

_____

_____

_____

A Grandmother's Life, as told to Her Grandchild
Teenage Years

During school hours some of my favorite activities or clubs I belonged to were _____

_____

_____

_____

Some of my favorite sports during high school were _____

_____

_____

_____

After school, I spent my time _____

_____

_____

_____

A Grandmother's Life, as told to Her Grandchild
Teenage Years

Some of my responsibilities at home were _____

_____

_____

_____

_____

My first summer job was _____

_____

_____

Other summer jobs I had were _____

_____

_____

_____

_____

A Grandmother's Life, as told to Her Grandchild
Teenage Years

and I also spent my summers _____

_____

_____

_____

_____

_____

_____

During high school, my favorite actors/actresses/musical groups were _____

_____

_____

_____

_____

_____

A Grandmother's Life, as told to Her Grandchild
Teenage Years

During high school, my favorite popular songs were _____

_____

_____

_____

_____

_____

As a teenager, I was beginning to formulate thoughts about myself. Some of them were _____

_____

_____

_____

_____

_____

A Grandmother's Life, as told to Her Grandchild
Teenage Years

As a teenager, I was beginning to formulate thoughts about life in general. Some of them were _____

_____

_____

_____

_____

_____

_____

As I became aware of politics, I could describe the political culture in our nation as _____

_____

_____

_____

_____

_____

_____

A Grandmother's Life, as told to Her Grandchild
Teenage Years

The religious climate in our nation could be described as _____

_____

_____

_____

My view of God could be described as _____

_____

_____

_____

_____

_____

_____

_____

A Grandmother's Life, as told to Her Grandchild
Teenage Years

and I could describe my spiritual awareness or faith as _____

_____

_____

_____

_____

MORE ABOUT MY TEENAGE YEARS: _____

_____

_____

_____

_____

_____

_____

_____

Grandmother's Life, as told to Her Grandchild

Teenage Years

Here's a picture of me as a teenager.

A Grandmother's Life, as told to Her Grandchild

Young Adult Years

A Grandmother's Life, as told to Her Grandchild

A Grandmother's Life, as told to Her Grandchild
Young Adult Years

Sometimes we are just going about our own business, living our daily lives, but because of where we live, we find we are part of a culture that is opposed to our beliefs. However, it is not a mistake. *God has placed us within the exact geographical border where He wants us to live.* "And He has made from one blood every nation of men to dwell on all the face of the earth, and has determined their pre-appointed times and the boundaries of their dwellings . . . " (Acts 17:26). Isn't that incredible! As astounding as that is, can you see how it is also comforting?

Esther was just an ordinary, young, Jewish woman whose life was turned upside down when she was challenged by her very own uncle to act upon her faith in the midst of a dangerous political situation. Perhaps she thought where she lived was a mistake. Yet, her life took an astonishing turn as she became a beauty queen in the King's court. She saved a nation and is considered a true heroine. God thought so highly of her that He wrote an entire book in the Bible about her life.

When I was a young adult, I could describe the political culture in our nation as _____

_____

_____

_____

_____

_____

A Grandmother's Life, as told to Her Grandchild
Young Adult Years

The religious climate in our nation when I was a young adult could be described as _____

_____

_____

_____

_____

_____

My dreams and aspirations as a young adult were _____

_____

_____

_____

_____

_____

A Grandmother's Life, as told to Her Grandchild
Young Adult Years

My best friend as a young adult was _____

and some of the things we did together were _____

_____

_____

_____

_____

The person who most influenced me while I was a young adult was _____

_____

Some of the ways I was impacted were _____

_____

_____

_____

_____

A Grandmother's Life, as told to Her Grandchild
Young Adult Years

I left my parents' home when I was _____ years old. I moved to _____

(City/State)

because _____

_____

_____

Some ways I viewed myself as a young adult were _____

_____

_____

_____

Some ways I viewed life as a young adult were _____

_____

_____

_____

A Grandmother's Life, as told to Her Grandchild
Young Adult Years

My formal education consisted of _____

_____

_____

_____

My view of God as a young adult could be described as _____

_____

_____

_____

and my spiritual life or faith could be described as _____

_____

_____

_____

MORE ABOUT MY YOUNG ADULT YEARS:

A Grandmother's Life, as told to Her Grandchild
Young Adult Years

Here's a picture of me as a young adult.

Mature Adult Years

A Grandmother's Life, as told to Her Grandchild

A Grandmother's Life, as told to Her Grandchild
Mature Adult Years

Job was an interesting character who was very vulnerable and upfront in his feelings towards God. God tested him and he questioned God. At the end of his trials, he realized that although he had heard *about* God, he didn't know him personally. Job received this wisdom after he had matured into an adult (Job 42:1-6).

Sometimes we do not have solid spiritual convictions until we have been tested by God through circumstances beyond our control.

But at the end of his life, God restored him physically, financially, emotionally, relationally and gave him a second family to enjoy. Job lived to be 140 years old and lived to participate in his second family's life, right down to four generations (Job 42.10-17).

What a joy it is to see one's children grow up. But to be able to live long enough to involve yourself in your grandchildren and great-grandchildren's lives — as Job did — that is an enormous blessing.

As I have matured, my dreams, hopes and goals have grown and changed. They could be described as _____

_____

_____

_____

_____

_____

A Grandmother's Life, as told to Her Grandchild
Mature Adult Years

As I have matured, my views about myself have changed from _____

_____

_____

_____

to _____

_____

_____

As I have matured, my views about life have also changed about _____

_____

_____

_____

A Grandmother's Life, as told to Her Grandchild
Mature Adult Years

The person(s) who most influenced me during my mature years was/were _____

_____

_____

Some of the ways I was impacted were _____

_____

_____

_____

The political culture in our nation has also changed. It could now be described as _____

_____

_____

_____

A Grandmother's Life as told to Her Grandchild
Mature Adult Years

The religious climate in our nation has changed too and could now be described as _____

My view about God and my spiritual life could be described as _____

A Grandmother's Life, as told to Her Grandchild
Mature Adult Years

As I have matured, some ways in which my spiritual convictions have grown and changed are _____

_____

_____

_____

_____

_____

_____

MORE ABOUT MY MATURE ADULT YEARS: _____

_____

_____

_____

_____

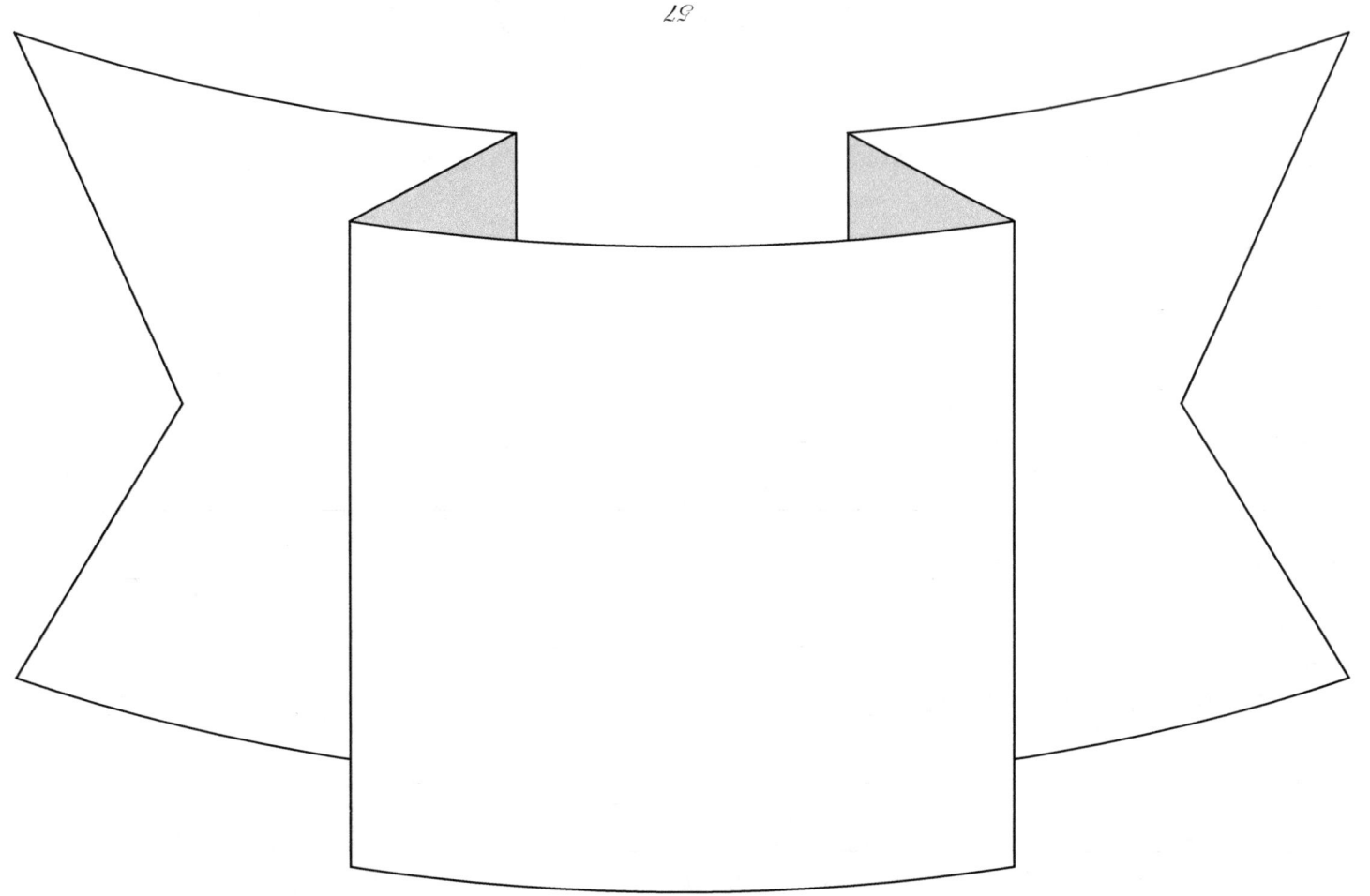

Grandmother's Life, as told to Her Grandchild

Mature Adult Years

Here's a picture of me as a more mature adult.

A Grandmother's Life, as told to Her Grandchild
Mature Adult Years

Years of Reflection

A Grandmother's Life, as told to Her Grandchild

A Grandmother's Life, as told to Her Grandchild
Years of Reflection

In Psalms 139:16 God says *He saw me even before I was born, and had already written down every single moment and every day of my life before it even happened.* Amazing isn't it? I find that hard to grasp, but it's true.

Job 14:5 says *He even decided how long I would live and where I would live before He created the world.* That's staggering to me. Although I wasn't always aware of God's influence, looking back, I can see His hand in many areas of my life.

As I reflect on my earlier dreams, hopes, goals, and aspirations, I _____

_____

_____

_____

_____

_____

Over all, the most influential person in my life was _____

because _____

_____

A Grandmother's Life, as told to Her Grandchild
Years of Reflection

Some other ways I was impacted were _____

_____

_____

_____

The most important practical lesson I learned was _____

_____

_____

_____

_____

The most unexpected life's lesson I learned was _____

_____

_____

_____

_____

A Grandmother's Life, as told to Her Grandchild
Years of Reflection

The greatest physical challenge I faced was _____

_____

_____

_____

_____

The greatest mental challenge I faced was _____

_____

_____

_____

_____

A Grandmother's Life, as told to Her Grandchild
Years of Reflection

The greatest emotional challenge I faced was _____

_____

_____

_____

_____

Looking back on the political culture of our nation and in the world during my lifetime, _____

_____

_____

_____

_____

_____

A Grandmother's Life, as told to Her Grandchild
Years of Reflection

As I reflect on the religious climate both in our nation and around the world during my lifetime, _____

_____

_____

_____

_____

_____

_____

MISCELLANEOUS RECOLLECTIONS:

The first time I saw snow fall I was _____ years old. I was in _____ and my
                                                                                (Location)

reaction was one of _____

_____

_____

A Grandmother's Life, as told to Her Grandchild
Years of Reflection

I experienced my first earthquake when I was _____ years old. I was in _____

(Location)

_____

and my reaction was one of _____

_____

_____

_____

I experienced my first hurricane/tornado/flood when I was _____ years old. I was in _____

(Location)

_____

and my reaction was one of _____

_____

_____

_____

A Grandmother's Life, as told to Her Grandchild
Years of Reflection

I saw the Pacific Ocean for the first time when I was _____ years old. I was in _____
                                                                                                                    (Location)

and my reaction was one of _____

_____

_____

_____

_____

I saw the Atlantic Ocean for the first time when I was _____ years old. I was in _____
                                                                                                                     (Location)

and my reaction was one of _____

_____

_____

_____

_____

A Grandmother's Life, as told to Her Grandchild
Years of Reflection

The most memorable vacation I ever took in my whole life was _____

_____

because _____

_____

_____

_____

A place I've always wanted to travel to and have never gone is _____

_____

because _____

_____

_____

_____

A Grandmother's Life, as told to Her Grandchild
Years of Reflection

I took my first airplane trip when I was _____ years old and went to _____

_____

_____

_____

I took my first train trip when I was _____ years old and went to _____

_____

_____

_____

A very special relative to me was my _____ named _____
                                                                 (Relationship)

He/she was special to me because _____

_____

_____

_____

A Grandmother's Life, as told to Her Grandchild
Years of Reflection

Some of my favorite colors are _____

_____

_____

_____

Some of my favorite foods as a child were _____

_____

_____

Some of my favorite foods as a teenager were _____

_____

_____

Some of my favorite foods as a young adult were _____

_____

_____

A Grandmother's Life, as told to Her Grandchild
Years of Reflection

I was _____ years old when I went on my first date. We _____

_____

_____

_____

_____

My first job after I finished my education was as a _____
                                                                                               (Title)

and my salary was _____. My responsibilities were _____
                       (Amount)

_____

_____

_____

_____

A Grandmother's Life, as told to Her Grandchild
Years of Reflection

I learned to drive at age _____ and the first car I drove was a _____
(Color/Year/Make/Model)

_____

The person(s) who taught me to drive was _____

_____

_____

I bought my first car in _____ and paid $_____. It was a _____
(Year)   (Color/Year/Make/Model)

At that time, gas cost _____ a gallon.

I bought my first house in _____ and paid $_____. It was located in _____
(Year)   (City/State)

I can still see it in my mind. I could describe it as _____

_____

_____

_____

A Grandmother's Life, as told to Her Grandchild
Years of Reflection

My lifetime hobbies have become _____

_____

_____

_____

Some ways/places I have volunteered for organizations have been _____

_____

_____

_____

LESSONS I HAVE LEARNED: _____

_____

_____

_____

WORDS OF WISDOM:

MORE REFLECTIONS:

A Grandmother's Life, as told to Her Grandchild

Special Memories

A Grandmother's Life, as told to Her Grandchild

A Grandmother's Life, as told to Her Grandchild
Special Memories

"But watch out! Be very careful never to forget what you have seen the Lord do for you. Do not let these things escape from your mind as long as you live! And be sure to pass them on to your children and grandchildren" (Deuteronomy 4:9).

Over and over God told the Israelites to remember: To specifically remember God—and to remember the good and the bad. When we remember good things, God refreshes us and we get another blessing when we bring back that memory. When we remember hard things, we can review the lessons we learned and do not have to repeat them. As I recall the following things, I am reminded of the good things in my life and of some harder lessons. But as God's child, He promises me ". . . that all things work together for good to them that love God, to them who are the called according to [his] purpose" (Romans 8:28). So no matter what I have experienced, I know God has used those things to develop me into the person He wants me to be. And I'm still being molded into what He wants me to be.

Your Grandfather and Me

I met your grandfather _____
(Name)

on _____ at _____
(Date)   (Event)

in _____
(City and State)

A Grandmother's Life, as told to Her Grandchild
Special Memories

My first impression was _____

_____

_____

_____

When we met, I was _____ years old and he was _____ years old, and I was attracted to him because _____

_____

_____

_____

At that time, your grandfather's occupation was _____

Or he was attending school at _____
(City and State)

When we met, my occupation was _____

Or I was attending school at _____
(City and State)

A Grandmother's Life, as told to Her Grandchild
Special Memories

We were married on _____ at _____
(City and State)

By then, I was _____ years old and he was _____ years old.

MORE ABOUT YOUR GRANDFATHER AND ME: _____

_____

_____

_____

_____

_____

_____

_____

_____

A Grandmother's Life, as told to Her Grandchild
Special Memories

Your Parent as a Child

My child _____ is your _____
              (First)   (Middle)   (Last)   (Father/Mother)

Your parent was named after _____

because _____

_____

_____

Your parent's name means _____

_____

Later your parent was nicknamed _____ by _____

because _____

_____

_____

A Grandmother's Life, as told to Her Grandchild
Special Memories

When your _____ was born, I was _____ years old.
　　　　　　(Father/Mother)

When I first held _____ I _____
　　　　　　　　　(him/her)

_____

_____

_____

When your _____ was growing up _____ always wanted to be a _____
　　　　　　(Father/Mother)　　　　　　　　　　　　(he/she)

_____

_____

because _____

_____

_____

A Grandmother's Life, as told to Her Grandchild
Special Memories

I thought your parent would grow up to be _____

_____

_____

because _____

_____

_____

_____

A special story I remember about your _____ when they were growing up was when _____
                                                    (Father/Mother)

_____

_____

_____

_____

A Grandmother's Life, as told to Her Grandchild
Special Memories

One of the funniest things I remember about your _____ was when _____
(Father/Mother)

_____

_____

_____

_____

_____

MORE ABOUT YOUR _____ WHEN _____ WAS A CHILD: _____
                       (Father/Mother)   (he/she)

_____

_____

_____

_____

_____

A Grandmother's Life, as told to Her Grandchild
Special Memories

Your Parents

Your parents met on _____ at _____
(Date)   (Event)

in _____
(City and State)

When they met, your father's occupation was _____

Or he was attending school at _____
(City and State)

and your mother's occupation was _____

Or she was attending school at _____
(City and State)

Your father was _____ years old and your mother was _____ years old.

I first met your future _____ at _____
(Father/Mother)   (Event)

in _____
(City and State)

A Grandmother's Life, as told to Her Grandchild
Special Memories

My first impression was _____

_____

_____

When your parents told me they were getting married, my response was _____

_____

_____

They established their first home in _____
(City/State)

MORE ABOUT YOUR PARENTS: _____

_____

_____

_____

_____

A Grandmother's Life, as told to Her Grandchild
Special Memories

Becoming Your Grandmother

When your parents told me they were expecting you, my grandchild, my reaction was _____

_____

_____

_____

When I became your grandmother I was _____ years old.

My vocation when you were born was _____

_____

The first time I saw you I was _____ years old, and we were at _____
(Location)

My first impression of you was _____

_____

_____

_____

A Grandmother's Life, as told to Her Grandchild
Special Memories

My spiritual life could be described as _____

_____

_____

_____

_____

_____

At that time, my views and ideas about being a grandmother were _____

_____

_____

_____

_____

_____

A Grandmother's Life, as told to Her Grandchild
Special Memories

Later those views and ideas changed. Now I look at being a grandmother as _____

_____

_____

_____

_____

_____

_____

_____

Sometimes little children cannot pronounce a grandmother's name clearly and as they grow up, they begin calling them another name.

The first name you called me was _____

Later you changed my name to _____

A Grandmother's Life, as told to Her Grandchild
Special Memories

MORE ABOUT BEING YOUR GRANDMOTHER: _____

Journey of Faith

A Grandmother's Life, as told to Her Grandchild

A Grandmother's Life, as told to Her Grandchild
Journey of Faith

The Psalmist said:
> O God, You have taught me from my youth;
> And to this day I declare Your wondrous works.
> Now also when I am old and grayheaded,
> O God, do not forsake me,
> Until I declare Your strength to this generation,
> Your power to everyone who is to come (Psalms 71:17-18).

I first became aware of my own personal journey of faith began when I was _____ years old. Like the psalmist, now that I am in my senior years, I deeply desire to declare and impart to you, my grandchild, some of what He has done in and through me.

Throughout my life, some places of worship I attended were _____

_____

_____

_____

My favorite pastor/minister/clergy was _____

because _____

_____

_____

A Grandmother's Life, as told to Her Grandchild
Journey of Faith

I was baptized/dedicated to the Lord at age _____ at _____
(Location)

Those present at the ceremony were _____

_____

_____

After the ceremony, we celebrated by _____

_____

_____

_____

I was baptized in water when I was _____ years old at _____
(Location)

Those present at the ceremony were _____

_____

_____

A Grandmother's Life, as told to Her Grandchild
Journey of Faith

After the ceremony, we celebrated by _____

_____

_____

_____

Later in life I made a personal profession of faith or committed my life to God when I was _____ years old at _____

_____
(Location)

Those who celebrated with me were _____

_____

_____

_____

The first prayer I ever learned/prayed was _____

_____

_____

A Grandmother's Life, as told to Her Grandchild

Journey of Faith

As a person grows, it is common to have questions about one's faith. I began to have those questions at age _____

Some things I questioned were

A Grandmother's Life, as told to Her Grandchild
Journey of Faith

I received my first Bible when I was _____ years old. It was given to me by _____
(Name)

_____

Our relationship was _____

_____

My favorite Bible verse is _____

because _____

_____

_____

_____

_____

_____

Grandmother's Life, as told to Her Grandchild
Journey of Faith

My life's verse is _____

because _____

I first realized what my life's verse was when _____

A Grandmother's Life, as told to Her Grandchild
Journey of Faith

I have seen this verse confirmed in my life through various means. Some ways are _____

_____

_____

_____

_____

_____

I discovered my spiritual gifts were _____

_____

_____

_____

_____

A Grandmother's Life, as told to Her Grandchild
Journey of Faith

Some of the ways I have used them in ministries were _____

_____

_____

_____

_____

_____

My spiritual passion is _____

_____

_____

_____

_____

A Grandmother's Life, as told to Her Grandchild
Journey of Faith

I discovered my spiritual calling was _____

and the way that calling developed over my lifetime has been _____

A Grandmother's Life, as told to Her Grandchild
Journey of Faith

Looking back on my spiritual life throughout my lifetime, the greatest spiritual challenge I faced was _____

_____

_____

_____

_____

MORE ABOUT MY JOURNEY OF FAITH: _____

_____

_____

_____

_____

_____

_____

A Grandmother's Life, as told to Her Grandchild
Journey of Faith

Proverbs 13:22, NLT says, "Good people leave an inheritance to their grandchildren, . . ." This is part of my inheritance to you. It does not tell you everything about me, but it will give you a lot of insight into who I am, and it may shed some light on why you are the way you are. It is my legacy, my personal inheritance for you, shared with much love.

The Psalmist Asaph expressed it this way:

> O my people, listen to my teaching. Open your ears to what I am saying, for I will speak to you in a parable. I will teach you hidden lessons from our past--stories we have heard and know, stories our ancestors handed down to us. We will not hide these truths from our children but will tell the next generation about the glorious deeds of the Lord. We will tell of his power and the mighty miracles he did. For he issued his decree to Jacob; he gave his law to Israel. He commanded our ancestors to teach them to their children, so the next generation might know them-even the children not yet born-that they in turn might teach their children. So each generation can set its hope anew on God, remembering his glorious miracles and obeying his commands (Psalms 78:1-8, NLT).